Introduction

Welcome to *The Accused Federal Guide to Justice: Immigration & ICE Survival Manual (Revised Edition)*

If you or a loved one is facing the threat of immigration detention, deportation, or navigating complex immigration proceedings—this manual is for you. The U.S. immigration system can be overwhelming, especially for individuals already entangled in the federal justice system or incarcerated in federal prison. This book was written to provide **clear, practical, and empowering information** for non-citizens caught between criminal and immigration law—commonly known as "crimmigration."

Unlike traditional legal texts, this guide breaks down the process in **plain English**, with a focus on what actually happens in real life—not just in legal theory. Whether you're facing an ICE arrest, detained while serving time in prison, or trying to help someone you love, this manual gives you tools, strategies, and clarity to understand your rights, prepare your defense, and protect your future

What This Book Offers

This manual covers **step-by-step guidance** on the following critical topics:

- **What Happens During an ICE Arrest or Encounter:**

Learn how ICE operates, what happens during an arrest, and how to handle questioning, paperwork, and your rights during an encounter.

- **Being Detained While Incarcerated:** Understand how ICE detainers work, when ICE can take custody from prison or jail, and how to prepare for that transition if you're currently serving a federal sentence.
- **How to Find Legal Help (Even If You Can't Afford It):** Tips on locating immigration attorneys, nonprofit legal organizations, and how to advocate for yourself in detention or court when resources are limited.
- **Bond Hearings and Requesting Release from Custody:** Know your options for getting out of ICE detention, including how to request a bond hearing, what the judge considers, and how to support your case.
- **Navigating the Immigration Court Process:** Learn about the two main types of hearings (Master Calendar and Individual), what to expect in court, and how to prepare for each step.
- **Asylum, Withholding, and Convention Against Torture (CAT) Claims:** Find out who qualifies for protection from

removal and how to file these complex but potentially life-saving applications.

- **Voluntary Departure vs. Removal Orders:** Explore the differences, pros and cons, and how each affects your ability to return to the U.S. in the future.
- **Appeals and Motions to Reopen:**
  Get the facts on what happens after a deportation order, and how to fight it with appeals to the Board of Immigration Appeals (BIA) or by filing a motion to reopen your case.

This book also includes **sample forms, legal templates, checklists, and a glossary** of commonly used immigration terms—so you're not left guessing what anything means.

Who Is This Manual For

- Individuals in **federal or local custody** who are not U.S. citizens
- People under ICE **investigation, arrest, or supervision**
- Families trying to help detained loved ones
- Advocates and case managers working with immigrant populations
- Anyone seeking to understand the immigration enforcement process in the U.S.

Whether you are just beginning your immigration case, are detained and fighting removal, or want to help someone in the system, this manual is here to serve as your **roadmap and resource.**

How to Use This Book

This manual is organized into clear sections that follow the timeline of what most people experience—from arrest, to detention, to court, and beyond. You don't need to read it all at once. Use the table of contents to go directly to the part you need most. Each chapter offers:

- A breakdown of key terms
- Real-world explanations
- Practical steps and options
- Tips for working with (or without) an attorney

There's no time to waste when dealing with immigration consequences—so let's get started.

Table of Contents

First Contact – How ICE Gets Involved

The U.S. Immigration and Customs Enforcement (ICE) plays a critical role in enforcing immigration laws within the United States. ICE involvement typically begins when a person is suspected of violating immigration laws or committing certain criminal offenses. Here's how the process works:

1. Initial Encounter or Identification

ICE often becomes involved through one of the following ways:

- **Criminal Arrests**: When someone is arrested by local or state law enforcement, ICE may be notified if the person is suspected of being undocumented or has prior immigration issues.
- **ICE Raids and Investigations:** ICE conducts workplace raids, home visits, and targeted enforcement actions to locate individuals believed to be in violation of immigration laws.
- **Immigration Applications and Background Checks**: Sometimes, individuals applying for immigration benefits (like a green card or visa extension) trigger an ICE review due to prior violations or incomplete paperwork.
- **Detainers (ICE Holds):** If a person is in jail, ICE can place an immigration detainer asking the facility to hold the individual for up to 48

hours after their scheduled release to allow ICE to take custody.

2. Detention and Processing

Once ICE takes custody, they will:

- Place the individual in an ICE detention facility or contract jail.
- Initiate removal (deportation) proceedings by filing a Notice to Appear (NTA) before an immigration judge.
- Determine eligibility for release on bond or parole, although in some cases, mandatory detention laws apply.

3. Removal Proceedings

During removal proceedings:

- ICE acts as the prosecuting agency, presenting the government's case for why the individual should be deported.
- The detained person may have a chance to fight their case in immigration court, applying for relief such as asylum, cancellation of removal, or adjustment of status.

4. Final Orders and Enforcement

If an immigration judge issues a final removal order:

- ICE is responsible for carrying out the deportation, which involves coordinating with the receiving country and arranging travel.
- In cases where removal is not immediately possible, ICE may have to release the individual under supervision, especially after six months, as clarified by Zadvydas v. Davis.

ICE's role is to locate, detain, and remove individuals who violate U.S. immigration laws. However, individuals have rights during this process, including the right to legal representation and, in some cases, the right to request bond or relief from deportation.

Chapter 1: ICE Encounters – When You Haven't Committed a Crime

1.1 – Who Is ICE and What Do They Do?

Immigration and Customs Enforcement (ICE) is a federal agency under the Department of Homeland Security (DHS), created in 2003 after the reorganization of federal agencies following the 9/11 attacks. ICE is responsible for enforcing immigration laws within the United States and has two primary divisions:

- **Enforcement and Removal Operations (ERO):** Locates, arrests, detains, and deports individuals who are in the U.S. unlawfully.
- **Homeland Security Investigations (HSI):** Focuses on serious cross-border crimes such as drug trafficking, cybercrimes, human trafficking, and visa fraud.

While HSI handles complex investigations, most immigration-related arrests are conducted by ERO agents.

1.2 – How Does ICE Know Who to Target?

ICE identifies individuals for enforcement using surveillance, public records, and interagency data-sharing. Key methods include:

- **Secure Communities Program:** Automatically shares biometric data (fingerprints) collected by local police with the FBI and ICE.

- **NCIC and FBI Databases:** Immigration violations and prior deportation orders often appear in these systems.
- **DMV and Public Records Access:** ICE may obtain driver's license and registration data.
- **Online Surveillance:** Social media and digital activity are monitored.
- **Public Tips:** ICE frequently receives anonymous tips from the public, employers, or law enforcement.

Case Reference: City of Los Angeles v. Barr (2020) demonstrates how federal-local cooperation impacts immigration enforcement.

1.3 – Arresting Someone Without a Crime

ICE can detain individuals without criminal charges because immigration violations are civil offenses. Common tools include:

- **Form I-200 (Administrative Arrest Warrant):** Signed by an ICE officer, not a judge.
- **Civil Standard of Proof:** Lower than criminal standards; no need for probable cause of a crime.

Under **8 U.S.C. § 1226** and **§ 1231**, ICE is legally authorized to detain individuals suspected of being removable.

Key Legal Cases: Galarza v. Szalczyk (2014), *Morales v. Chadbourne* (2015)

1.4 – How an ICE Arrest Happens

ICE encounters can happen in several settings:

- **At Home or Work:** Often early morning visits; agents may use deception to gain entry.
- **Courthouses:** Common in non-cooperative jurisdiction despite legal challenges.
- **Public Spaces:** ICE makes arrests during traffic stops and in public areas.

Without a judicial warrant, ICE cannot legally enter a home without consent. Remain silent; your administrative warrant alone is not sufficient.

1.5 – What to Say and Do During an ICE Encounter

Here are **key rights and strategies** to use if someone is stopped by ICE:

✅ **Do:**

- **Stay calm.**
- Ask if you are free to leave. If they say yes, leave calmly.
- Exercise your **right to remain silent.**
- Say: "I am exercising my right to remain silent and want to speak to a lawyer."

- **Refuse to sign** any documents, especially if you don't understand them.
- Ask to see any **warrant or paperwork.**

✕ Don't:

- Don't lie or provide false documents.
- Don't run—this may be used against you in immigration court.
- Don't open the door unless they present a **judicial warrant** with your full name signed by a judge.

Chapter 2: ICE Detainers – When You've Been Charged or Convicted of a Crime

2.1 – What Is an ICE Detainer? An ICE detainer is a request to a law enforcement agency to notify ICE of a noncitizen's pending release and to hold the person for up to 48 hours so ICE can assume custody.

- Form I-247A: Used to issue detainers.
- Detainers are not judicial warrants and are considered voluntary by many jurisdictions.

Legal Basis: 8 C.F.R. §287.7(d)

Key Cases: Galarza v. Szalczyk (2014), Morales v. Chadbourne (2015)

1. Galarza v. Szalczyk (3d Cir. 2014)

Citation: 745 F.3d 634 (3d Cir. 2014)

Background:

Ernesto Galarza, a U.S. citizen born in New Jersey, was arrested in Pennsylvania on drug charges. Despite posting bail, he remained detained for three days due to an ICE detainer, which was based on the mistaken belief that he was not a U.S. citizen. Temple University Beasley School of Law

Key Ruling:

The Third Circuit Court of Appeals held that ICE detainers are **voluntary requests**, not mandatory orders. Therefore, local law enforcement agencies are **not obligated** to comply with them. The court emphasized that detaining someone solely based on an ICE detainer, without independent probable cause, can violate the individual's Fourth Amendment rights.

Impact:

This decision clarified that local and state authorities could be held liable for unlawfully detaining individuals based solely on ICE detainers. It underscored the importance of verifying an individual's citizenship status and the necessity of probable cause before detention.

2. Morales v. Chadbourne (1st Cir. 2015)

Citation: 793 F.3d 208 (1st Cir. 2015)

Background:

Ada Morales, a naturalized U.S. citizen from Guatemala, was arrested in Rhode Island. Despite informing authorities of her citizenship and offering to show her naturalization documents, she was detained for 24 hours under an ICE detainer.

Key Ruling:

The First Circuit Court of Appeals ruled that detaining an individual based solely on an ICE detainer, without **probable cause**, violates the Fourth Amendment. The court emphasized that immigration officials must have probable cause to issue a detainer and that detaining someone without it is unconstitutional.

Impact:

This case reinforced the principle that U.S. citizens cannot be detained without probable cause, even in immigration-related matters. It highlighted the potential for constitutional violations when ICE detainers are issued without proper verification and legal basis.

Summary:

Both cases underscore the importance of constitutional protections against unlawful detention. They clarify that:

- ICE detainers are **requests**, not mandates.
- Local and state authorities are **not required** to honor ICE detainers without an independent probable cause.

- Detaining individuals, especially U.S. citizens, without probable cause based on ICE detainers can lead to violations of the Fourth Amendment.vLex+9American Civil Liberties Union+9ACLU Pennsylvania+9ACLU Pennsylvania

These rulings have significant implications for immigration enforcement practices and the rights of individuals within the U.S.

2.2 – How ICE Finds Out About Inmates Through programs such as:

- Secure Communities: Biometrics shared from jails trigger ICE notification.
- Criminal Alien Program (CAP): Allows ICE agents to work inside jails and screen individuals.

Statute: 8 U.S.C. §1373 (modified in recent litigation, including City of Chicago v. Sessions)

2.3 – From Prison to ICE Custody ICE typically waits until the completion of a sentence before taking custody:

- BOP and ICE Coordination: ICE is notified in advance of release.
- Post-Release Transfer: Detainees may be transferred directly into ICE detention facilities.

2.4 – The Legal Trap: Double Punishment Serving a criminal sentence does not end legal jeopardy for immigrants. After completing a sentence, individuals may:

- Face immediate ICE detention.
- Be subject to mandatory detention under 8 U.S.C. §1226(c).

Demore v. Kim *(538 U.S. 510 2003),* ***Zadvydas v. Davis*** *533 U.S. 678 G (2001)* clarified the legality of mandatory and prolonged detention.

1. **Zadvydas v. Davis** (2001)

- **Issue:**
  Whether the government can indefinitely detain immigrants with final removal orders when their removal is not reasonably foreseeable (e.g., no country will accept them).
- **Ruling:**
  The Supreme Court held that indefinite detention is unconstitutional under the Due Process Clause of the Fifth Amendment.
- **Key Point:**
  The Court set a presumptive limit of six months for detention after a final removal order. If the government cannot show that removal is likely in the foreseeable future, the detainee must be released.

- **Impact:**
  This case protects individuals from being locked up indefinitely when deportation is not realistically possible.

2. **Demore v. Kim** (2003)

- **Issue:**
  Whether the government can mandatorily detain lawful permanent residents (LPRs) who have committed certain crimes while their removal proceedings are pending, without a bond hearing.
- **Ruling:**
  The Supreme Court upheld the government's authority under 8 U.S.C. § 1226(c) to mandatorily detain certain noncitizens without a bond hearing during their removal proceedings.
- **Key Point:**
  The Court reasoned that this detention is typically brief and limited to the duration of removal proceedings, which they assumed would not last long.
- **Impact:**
  This ruling allows for mandatory detention of certain criminal noncitizens, even if they are lawful permanent residents, during pending deportation proceedings.

Summary of the Two Cases Together:

- **Zadvydas v. Davis** (2001): Protects against indefinite detention after a final removal order.
- **Demore v. Kim** (2003): Allows for mandatory detention without bond hearings during removal proceedings, especially for certain criminal offenses.

Additional Resources:

- American Immigration Council: https://www.americanimmigrationcouncil.org/
- National Immigration Project: https://nipnlg.org/
- ACLU on Detainers: https://www.aclu.org/issues/immigrants-rights/ice-and-border-patrol-abuses/ice-detainers

2.5 – Rights While in ICE Custody and Preparing for the Next Step

Once transferred into ICE custody, detainees have specific rights under both immigration regulations and the U.S. Constitution, even though removal proceedings are civil in nature. These rights include:

- The Right to Due Process: Individuals have the right to challenge their detention and removal in immigration court.
- The Right to Legal Representation (at one's own expense): Unlike criminal cases, there is no public defender system in immigration court, but individuals may hire or seek pro bono immigration counsel.
- The Right to Request a Bond Hearing (if eligible): Not all detainees qualify for bond, especially those subject to mandatory detention.
- Right to remain silent and not self-incriminate
- Right to contact your consulate
- Right to legal representation (at your own expense)
- Access to law library and legal materials
- Right to receive a Notice to Appear (NTA)
- Right to a bond hearing (in many cases)
- Medical care and humane conditions
- Special considerations for asylum seekers and vulnerable populations
- Preparing documents and evidence for your case

- Communicating with family and support networks
- Understanding the next steps: Removal proceedings, voluntary departure, or release
- Planning for post-release or deportation outcomes

Detainee Rights: Communicating with Your Consulate

Your Right to Contact Your Consulate

If you're not a U.S. citizen and you're detained by immigration authorities, **you have the right to contact your country's consulate**. This right is protected under both U.S. law and international treaties — and it's a big deal.

When ICE detains a non-citizen, they are *supposed* to inform you that you can request contact with your consulate. This is **not just a courtesy** — it's a legal right. Some countries even have agreements with the U.S. where ICE must notify the consulate automatically, no matter what.

So, what does this mean for you as a detainee?

- **You can ask to speak with a representative of your country's consulate.**

- **You can request help from them.** That includes:
    - Notifying your family back home,
    - Helping with legal representation,
    - Assisting with language translation or communication barriers,
    - Ensuring you're treated fairly under both U.S. and international law.

Tip: If ICE doesn't tell you about your consular rights, or they block you from making contact, that can potentially be used later as a violation of due process. It won't automatically get your case dismissed, but it can matter during appeals or motions.

What's the Vienna Convention All About?

Now let's clear the air on something you've probably heard but might not have fully understood — **the Vienna Convention on Consular Relations (1963)**.

This treaty is like a worldwide agreement between over 180 countries, including the United States. It sets the rules on how countries treat foreign nationals, especially when they're **arrested, detained, or imprisoned** in a country that's not their own.

Key takeaway?
Under Article 36 of the Vienna Convention, when someone is arrested in a foreign country, the authorities **must inform them of their right to contact their consulate.** It's about protecting

individuals so they're not isolated or left in the dark just because they're not in their home country.

Here's why it's important:

- It's **an international promise**: Countries agreed to follow these rules so their citizens would be protected when abroad.
- It **reinforces fairness**: Language barriers, cultural confusion, and legal unfamiliarity can leave non-citizens vulnerable. The consulate helps bridge that gap.
- It **can impact your case**: If your right to consular notification was violated, it could play a role in appeals or arguments about fairness and due process.

  In other words, **the Vienna Convention exists to make sure nobody is left helpless in a foreign legal system.** It's about mutual respect between countries — "We protect your people, you protect ours."
- Stay Informed: Individuals should be given a Notice to Appear (NTA), which outlines the charges and upcoming court dates.

Key Case Reference:

- *Rodriguez v. Robbins* (2013) established the importance of timely bond hearings, though later narrowed by *Jennings v. Rodriguez* (2018), which ruled that immigrants in prolonged detention do not have a statutory right to periodic bond hearings.(See in more details below.

Rodriguez v. Robbins (715 F.3d. 1127 9th Cir. 2013) – Immigrant Rights to Timely Bond Hearings

In *Rodriguez v. Robbins*, the Ninth Circuit ruled that **immigrants detained for prolonged periods (over six months)** under mandatory detention provisions were entitled to **automatic bond hearings every six months**. The court held that prolonged detention without a bond hearing raised serious **constitutional due process concerns**.

This case was important for protecting immigrant rights by ensuring that individuals in long-term detention could argue for their release before an immigration judge, rather than being held indefinitely.

Jennings v. Rodriguez (No. 15-1204 U.S. Supreme Court 2018) – No Automatic Right to Bond Hearings

In *Jennings v. Rodriguez*, the U.S. Supreme Court overturned the Ninth Circuit's decision. The Court held that **federal immigration laws (8 U.S.C. §§ 1225(b), 1226(a), and 1226(c)) do not require periodic bond hearings**, even for long-term detainees.

The Court rejected the idea that bond hearings were automatically required after six months of detention. It stated that the statute's language did not support this requirement, and courts could not "rewrite" the law to impose such a rule.

Conflict Between the Two Rulings

- *Rodriguez v. Robbins* prioritized **due process and constitutional protections**, giving immigrants a chance to argue for their release during prolonged detention.
- *Jennings v. Rodriguez* focused strictly on the **statutory language**, concluding that immigrants **do not have a constitutional or statutory right to automatic bond hearings**, even during long-term detention.

  In simple terms, the Ninth Circuit tried to protect detainees' rights under constitutional principles, but the Supreme Court overruled that approach, emphasizing that **Congress did not guarantee such rights in the immigration statutes**.

Helpful Resources:

- EOIR (Executive Office for Immigration Review): https://www.justice.gov/eoir

- Immigration Advocates Network: https://www.immigrationadvocates.org/
- Detention Watch Network: https://www.detentionwatchnetwork.org/

Chapter 3: Finding Legal Help & Bond

3.1 – Understanding the Importance of Legal Representation

Navigating immigration proceedings without a lawyer is extremely difficult. A qualified attorney can:

- Explain your rights and legal options.
- Represent you at bond hearings and in court.
- Prepare evidence and legal motions that may lead to release or relief from removal.

Tip: Immigration court does not provide free attorneys. You must secure your own legal representation.

3.2 – Locating Legal Assistance

Many nonprofit organizations and pro bono attorneys offer free or low-cost legal help. Search legal directories like immigrationadvocates.org to find resources in your area.

3.3 – Preparing for Bond Hearings

A bond hearing is your chance to argue for release from ICE custody. The judge considers:

- Flight risk and public safety concerns.
- Ties to the U.S. (family, work, community).
- Criminal history and rehabilitation.

What to Prepare:

- Letters of support from family, employers, and community leaders.
- Proof of residence and employment.
- Records of good behavior.

3.4 – Nationwide Organizations Offering Legal Aid

- **National Immigration Legal Services Directory** – immigrationadvocates.org
- **National Immigrant Justice Center (NIJC)** – immigrantjustice.org

- **Freedom for Immigrants** – freedomforimmigrants.org
- **Legal Orientation Program (LOP)** – justice.gov/eoir

1. Understanding the Importance of Legal Representation

Legal representation is one of the most critical components of navigating the federal justice system. An experienced attorney can help ensure your constitutional rights are protected, advise you on the strength of your case, negotiate plea deals, and prepare for trial or sentencing. Even if you plan to pursue self-representation (pro se), consulting a lawyer for strategic advice is highly recommended.

2. Locating Legal Assistance

Finding the right legal help can be challenging, especially for those with limited financial resources. Start by contacting your local public defender's office if you have not been assigned counsel. You may also reach out to legal clinics, law school programs, or nonprofit organizations that provide pro bono services. If you are detained, request a legal aid directory from the facility's law library or case manager.

3. Preparing for Bond Hearings

A bond hearing determines whether you will be released while awaiting trial. Preparation is crucial. You should gather the following:

- Proof of community ties (letters from family, employers, clergy)
- Proof of stable residence
- Employment or school enrollment documentation
- A release plan with supervision if required
  Having an attorney present can significantly increase your chances of being granted bond. If denied, you can request a bond review hearing at a later time.

4. Nationwide Organizations Offering Legal Aid
There are several reputable organizations that offer legal help to individuals in federal custody or immigration proceedings:

- **The Innocence Project** – Focuses on wrongful convictions
- **National Legal Aid & Defender Association (NLADA)** – Provides a directory of local services
- **American Civil Liberties Union (ACLU)** – Litigates constitutional rights violations
- **Catholic Legal Immigration Network (CLINIC)** – Offers immigration legal support
- **Federal Public Defender Offices** – Available in every federal district

Georgia-Based Legal Aid
If you are located in Georgia or have a pending case there, consider contacting these resources:

- **Georgia Legal Services Program** – Offers free legal aid to low-income residents
- **Atlanta Legal Aid Society** – Assists with civil and criminal matters
- **Southern Center for Human Rights** – Focuses on justice system reform and representation for indigent clients
- **Georgia Innocence Project** – Works to exonerate the wrongfully convicted
- **State Bar of Georgia Pro Bono Project** – Connects individuals with volunteer attorneys

📋 Bond Hearing Preparation Checklist

Item	Description	Attached?
Valid Address	Where you will stay if released	☐
Letter from Employer	Verifying job availability	☐
Letters of Support	At least 2-3 strong letters	☐
Community Involvement	Church, volunteer, etc.	☐

Item	Description	Attached?
Birth Certificates	For children/spouse	☐
Legal Brief (if possible)	Written argument from lawyer	☐

▮ Template: Letter of Support for Bond Hearing

[Your Full Name]

[Address]

[Phone Number]

[Date]

To Whom It May Concern:

I am writing in support of [Detainee's Full Name], who is currently in immigration detention. I have known them for [X years] and can speak to their good character and positive role in our community.

[Insert personal story or relationship.]

If released, [Name] has a safe home to return to at [Address] and will attend all scheduled court hearings.

Sincerely,

[Your Signature]

[Your Name]

Here's a more detailed directory of **trusted organizations** helping people in ICE detention with bond hearings and general immigration defense:

☐☐ **National Immigrant Justice Center (NIJC)**

- **Services**: Representation for detained individuals, bond advocacy
- **Phone**: (773) 672-6599 | Detention line: (312) 583-9721 (accepts collect calls)
- **Website**: immigrantjustice.org

□ **Freedom for Immigrants**

- **Services**: Bond fund referrals, legal helpline, detention maps.
- **Phone**: (209) 757-3733
- **Website**: freedomforimmigrants.org

⚖□ **Catholic Legal Immigration Network, Inc. (CLINIC)**

- **Services**: Training and support for legal nonprofits nationwide.
- **Website**: cliniclegal.org

□ **RAICES (Texas)**

- **Services**: Legal services and bond assistance for ICE detainees.
- **Phone**: (210) 222-0964
- **Website**: raicestexas.org

Winning a bond hearing gets you released, but **your immigration case still continues**. You must:

- Keep your address updated with the court and ICE.
- Show up to all hearings.
- Keep working with your attorney to fight your case or seek relief.

Pro Tip: Bond Hearings Are Just the Start

Winning a bond hearing gets you released, but your immigration case still continues. You must:

- Keep your address updated with the court and ICE.
- Show up to all hearings.
- Keep working with your attorney to fight your case or seek relief.

Frequently Asked Questions from Real Detainees

Q1: Can I have a bond hearing if I have a criminal record? A: Yes, but it depends on the type of offense. Some crimes make you ineligible for bond. Speak to a qualified attorney to determine your options.

Q2: What happens if I lose my bond hearing? A: You can file a request for a new hearing if circumstances change or appeal to the Board of Immigration Appeals (BIA).

Q3: How much is a typical bond amount? A: Bonds can range from $1,500 to over $25,000. The judge will consider your ties to the community, employment, and criminal history.

Q4: Can family members pay the bond? A: Yes, a family member or friend with legal status can pay your bond at an ICE-approved facility using a cashier's check or money order.

Q5: What if I can't afford the bond? A: Look into bond assistance programs like those through Freedom for Immigrants or local immigrant rights groups.

Q6: How can I prepare if I don't have a lawyer? A: Gather documents, ask family for letters, and practice telling your story clearly. Use legal aid directories to find free or low-cost support.

Tips on Working with Public Defenders

If you are assigned a public defender or court-appointed attorney in any part of your case:

- **Be honest and clear.** Share all facts—even if they seem negative. Surprises hurt cases.
- **Ask questions.** Don't be afraid to ask for explanations or updates.
- **Stay organized.** Keep copies of paperwork and share documents with your attorney.
- **Follow their advice.** Public defenders know the legal system and can guide you wisely, even under tight timeframes.

Remember: immigration court doesn't automatically assign public defenders. But if you're also facing criminal charges, you might have one—and your immigration attorney can coordinate with them.

Can Paralegals Help?

Yes—especially when supervised by an attorney or working with an accredited organization. Paralegals can:

- Help prepare forms and bond packets.
- Assist in writing letters, organizing evidence, or gathering supporting documents.
- Conduct legal research under attorney supervision.
- Explain procedures and timelines in simpler terms.

Look for paralegals trained in immigration law or who work with recognized nonprofits. Never pay large sums for paralegal services without verifying their credentials or connection to a legitimate legal organization.

Callout: Watch Out for Immigration Fraud

Warning Signs of Fake Legal Help:

- Someone asking for money with no contract or receipt.

- Promising "guaranteed" results or outcomes.
- Notaries (notarios) or individuals claiming to be "immigration consultants" without legal accreditation.
- Anyone unwilling to give you a copy of your documents or filing receipts.

Always verify a lawyer's bar number or a representative's DOJ accreditation: EOIR Attorney Listing

Trusted Paralegal and Legal Aid Programs

Certain programs and nonprofit organizations train and certify paralegals to assist immigrants under the supervision of licensed attorneys. Look for these trusted sources:

- **Immigrant Legal Resource Center (ILRC)** – Provides training for accredited representatives and legal workers.
    - ilrc.org
- **National Immigration Project (NIPNLG)** – Connects legal support with experienced advocates.
    - nipnlg.org
- **Catholic Charities Legal Services** – Offers paralegal and attorney-based support for low-income clients.

- Search for your local Catholic Charities office online.

Paralegals: Affordable but Limited

Benefits of Using a Paralegal:

- **Lower Cost**: Paralegals often charge much less than attorneys, especially for basic document prep.
- **Document Support**: They can help fill out immigration forms, write letters, organize evidence, and prepare bond packets.
- **Clear Communication**: Paralegals often explain things in a more understandable way.

Downsides and Limits:

- **Not Authorized to Represent in Court**: Paralegals cannot argue your case before a judge or attend bond hearings unless under direct supervision.
- **May Not Provide Legal Advice**: They can't legally offer advice unless part of a DOJ-recognized organization.
- **Quality Varies**: Without oversight, some may overpromise and underdeliver.

Pro Tip: Always Ask

Before hiring a paralegal, ask:

- Are you working under a licensed attorney or DOJ-accredited organization?
- Can you provide receipts and contracts?
- Have you worked on immigration bond cases before?

A trustworthy paralegal will always answer these questions clearly and provide documentation.

Understanding the Immigration Court Process

Once detained or placed in removal proceedings, you will receive a Notice to Appear (NTA), which starts the formal court process. Here is what to expect:

Step-by-Step Overview:

- **Notice to Appear (NTA)**: Lists the charges and why the government believes you should be removed.
- **Master Calendar Hearing (MCH)**: A brief hearing where you confirm or deny charges and tell the judge what relief you're seeking.
- **Individual Hearing (Merits Hearing)**: You present your full case, with witnesses, documents, and testimony. The judge will decide whether you can stay or be deported.
- can appeal this decision within 30 days.

- **Board of Immigration Appeals (BIA)**: Handles appeals of immigration judge decisions. Must be filed within deadlines and often requires strong legal writing.

Key Tips:

- Always attend your hearings. Missing one can result in an automatic removal order.
- Dress neatly and show respect to the judge and courtroom.
- Bring all documents and evidence to each hearing.

Understanding the Immigration Court Process

- **Notice to Appear (NTA)**
  The immigration process begins when a person receives a **Notice to Appear**, a legal document that lists the charges for removal and the reasons the U.S. government believes the individual should be deported. The NTA requires the person to appear before an immigration judge on a specific date.

- **Master Calendar Hearing**
  This is the first hearing in immigration court. It's usually brief and includes multiple cases scheduled for the same day. The judge explains the charges and asks how the individual pleads. If they don't have a lawyer,

they can ask for more time to get one. No final decisions are made at this hearing unless the person admits to the charges and waives further proceedings.

- **Individual Hearing**
  This is a longer, one-on-one hearing where the person presents their full case before the judge. Evidence is introduced, witnesses may testify, and the government will argue for removal. The judge can decide the case at the end of the hearing or take more time to issue a written decision.

- **Board of Immigration Appeals (BIA)**
  If the immigration judge issues a removal order, the individual can appeal the decision to the **Board of Immigration Appeals**. The BIA reviews the case record and determines whether the judge made any legal or procedural errors. Appeals must be filed within 30 days of the judge's decision.

Chapter 4: Types of Relief from Removal (Deportation)

In this chapter, we will cover all the major types of legal relief available to noncitizens facing deportation. These forms of relief could stop or delay removal and may even lead to permanent lawful status. This chapter is designed to help both detainees and their families understand all their options.

Section 1: Asylum, Withholding of Removal, and CAT (Convention Against Torture)

Asylum

- Protects individuals who fear persecution in their home country because of:
  - Race
  - Religion
  - Nationality
  - Political opinion
  - Membership in a particular social group
- Must file within 1 year of arrival in the U.S. (exceptions may apply)
- Benefits: Work authorization, path to green card

Sample Case: Maria from Honduras

Maria fled domestic violence and threats from a gang. She applied for asylum within a year of entry. Her lawyer helped her gather police reports, witness affidavits, and psychological evaluations. She was granted asylum after her individual hearing.

Lawyer/Paralegal Tips:

- Help detainees complete Form I-589.
- Gather evidence: photos, country reports, affidavits.
- Prepare the client for testimony on trauma.

Withholding of Removal

- Similar to asylum, but harder to win
- Requires showing a "clear probability" of persecution
- No path to green card, but protects from deportation

CAT (Convention Against Torture)

- For those likely to be tortured if returned to their country
- No green card, but provides protection

Common Mistakes:

- Missing the 1-year deadline for asylum

- Weak documentation of threats or past harm

Section 2: Cancellation of Removal

For Lawful Permanent Residents (LPRs)

- Requirements:
    - 7 years of continuous residence
    - 5 years as a green card holder
    - No aggravated felony convictions

For Non-LPRs (undocumented or visa overstays)

- **Requirements:**
    - 10 years in the U.S.
    - Good moral character
    - U.S. citizen or LPR spouse/child/parent would suffer "exceptional and extremely unusual hardship"

Sample Case: Juan, LPR for 6 years

Juan had a green card and two U.S. citizen children. After a minor drug offense, ICE began removal proceedings. His lawyer proved he had over 7 years in the U.S. and no aggravated felony. His removal was cancelled.

Paralegal Prep Tips:

- Assist in collecting tax records, school records, and letters of support.
- Draft personal declarations and hardship statements.

Common Mistakes:

- Assuming minor crimes are not deportable offenses
- Not providing enough proof of hardship

Section 3: Adjustment of Status, U Visas, and Other Forms

Adjustment of Status

- Some may apply for a green card through family or employment
- Must be eligible through an approved petition (e.g., I-130)

U Visa (for crime victims)

- Victims of serious crimes who help law enforcement

T Visa (for human trafficking victims)

- Must show you were trafficked and helped law enforcement

Special Immigrant Juvenile Status (SIJS)

- For children abused, neglected, or abandoned

VAWA (Violence Against Women Act)

- For victims of abuse by a U.S. citizen or LPR

Sample Case: Sara, Domestic Violence Survivor

Sara's LPR husband abused her and threatened deportation. With paralegal help, she filed a VAWA petition and obtained work authorization and later a green card.

Paralegal Tips:

- Prepare affidavits and gather supporting evidence.
- Help complete Form I-918 (U Visa), I-360 (VAWA), or I-485 (Adjustment).

Common Mistakes:

- Not reporting the crime to law enforcement (U Visa issue)
- Missing supporting documents for VAWA cases

Section 4: Voluntary Departure vs. Removal Orders

Voluntary Departure

- You agree to leave the U.S. at your own expense
- Avoids a formal removal order

Removal Order

- Judge orders deportation
- Can trigger 5–10-year reentry bans

Legal Strategy Tip:

- Paralegals can draft voluntary departure requests to preserve reentry options
- Lawyers may negotiate with DHS for voluntary departure instead of full removal

Section 5: Appeals and Motions

Board of Immigration Appeals (BIA)

- Must appeal within 30 days

Motion to Reopen

- New facts or circumstances changed

Motion to Reconsider

- Based on legal errors in the judge's decision

Case Example: Karim, Asylum Denied

Karim lost his asylum case but learned new evidence became available. A paralegal helped his attorney file a motion to reopen based on country condition changes.

Eligibility Tip Chart

Form of Relief	Good For...	Key Requirement(s)
Asylum	Fear of persecution	Must apply within 1 year
Cancellation (LPR)	Green card holders	5 years LPR, 7 years residence
Cancellation (Non-LPR)	Undocumented immigrants	10 years, hardship to family
U Visa	Crime victims	Assisted law enforcement
VAWA	Abuse victims	Abuse by U.S. citizen or LPR
Adjustment of Status	Family-sponsored cases	Must have valid petition
CAT	Fear of torture	Must show likelihood of torture

This chapter is meant to be a powerful roadmap. For many, a knowledgeable paralegal or legal advocate, which may be the only hope to prepare properly. Always verify credentials and gather strong documentation early.

Forms of Immigration Relief

Asylum, Withholding of Removal, and CAT (Convention Against Torture)

Asylum protects individuals who fear persecution in their home country based on race, religion, nationality, political opinion, or membership in a particular social group. It must generally be filed within one year of entering the U.S.

Withholding of Removal is similar to asylum but has a higher burden of proof and does not lead to a green card. It prevents deportation to a country where the person's life or freedom would be threatened.

Convention Against Torture (CAT) provides protection to individuals who can prove they would likely be tortured by or with the consent of their home country's government. Unlike asylum, CAT relief is not based on personal identity categories.

Cancellation of Removal

This is a defense against deportation that allows some non-citizens to remain in the U.S. if they meet specific requirements. For undocumented immigrants, they must prove they've been in the U.S. for at least 10 years, have good moral character, and their removal would cause exceptional hardship to a U.S. citizen or permanent resident spouse, parent, or child.

Adjustment of Status, U Visas, and Other Forms

- **Adjustment of Status** allows certain individuals to apply for lawful permanent residence (green card) without leaving the U.S.
- **U Visas** are for victims of certain crimes who have helped law enforcement. This visa can lead to permanent residency.
- **Other forms** of relief include T Visas for trafficking victims, VAWA petitions for abused spouses or children of U.S. citizens or residents, and SIJS (Special Immigrant Juvenile Status) for abused, neglected, or abandoned minors.

Voluntary Departure vs. Removal Orders

Voluntary Departure allows someone to leave the U.S. on their own within a set time frame without a formal removal order, which may help avoid long-term bars to reentry.

Removal Orders are issued by an immigration judge and result in formal deportation, which can carry penalties such as bans on returning to the U.S. for 5, 10, or 20 years—or even permanently in some cases.

Appeals and Motions for Immigration Proceedings (reiterated)

Appeals

If an immigration judge issues a decision—such as a removal order—the individual has the right to **appeal** to the **Board of Immigration Appeals (BIA)**. The appeal must be filed within **30 days** of the judge's decision. The BIA reviews legal errors, not new evidence, and can uphold, reverse, or send the case back (remand) to the judge for further proceedings.

Motions to Reopen

A **Motion to Reopen** asks the immigration court to review the case again due to new evidence or changed circumstances that were not available during the original hearing. For example, new asylum claims, new documentation, or a change in the law. This motion must usually be filed within **90 days** of the final order—unless based on exceptional circumstances or filed by the government.

Motions to Reconsider

A **Motion to Reconsider** asks the court to reevaluate its decision based on legal errors in the original ruling. It does not introduce new evidence but argues that the judge misapplied the law or facts. It must generally be filed within **30 days** of the decision.

Stay of Removal

While an appeal or motion is pending, an individual can request a **Stay of Removal**, which is a temporary pause on deportation. A stay is not automatic and must be requested from the court or the Department of Homeland Security (DHS).

Chapter 5: Asylum Claims

This chapter focuses specifically on asylum—one of the most important protections available in U.S. immigration law. It is a lifeline for individuals fleeing serious danger in their home countries. In this chapter, we break down the process, offer case examples, provide tips for legal preparation, and explore common mistakes and legal strategies.

Section 1: What Is Asylum?

1. **Definition**
   - Asylum is a legal protection for individuals who have suffered persecution or fear future persecution based on:
     - Race
     - Religion
     - Nationality
     - Political opinion
     - Membership in a particular social group
2. **Types of Asylum Claims**
   - *Affirmative*: Applied for outside removal proceedings
   - *Defensive*: Applied for as a defense against removal

Section 2: Who Qualifies for Asylum?

1. **Eligibility Criteria**
   - Physical presence in the U.S.

- Application filed within 1 year of arrival (some exceptions apply)
- Must prove credible fear of persecution

2. **Barriers to Eligibility**
    - Serious criminal convictions
    - Participation in persecution of others
    - Safe third country agreement (rare)

Section 3: The Asylum Process (Step-by-Step)

1. **Filing the Application**
    - Form I-589, filed with USCIS (affirmative) or EOIR (defensive)
    - No fee required
2. **Credible Fear Interview (CFI)**
    - For detainees who express fear when apprehended
    - Must establish a significant possibility of persecution
3. **Immigration Court Hearing**
    - Presentation of evidence and testimony
    - Opportunity to cross-examine government witnesses
4. **Final Decision**

- Judge grants or denies asylum; denial can be appealed to BIA

Section 4: Case Examples

- **Case 1: Gender-Based Violence**
  Luz from Guatemala fled severe domestic violence. She filed within the deadline and included psychological records and country conditions. Judge granted asylum.

: Case Examples

- A young woman fleeing gang violence in Honduras because of her gender and resistance to forced recruitment was granted asylum under "membership in a particular social group."
- A journalist from Eritrea was granted asylum for political opinion after being imprisoned and tortured for writing anti-government articles.
- A gay man from Uganda received asylum due to severe persecution based on sexual orientation, protected under "particular social group."
- **Case 2: Political Opinion**
  Ahmed from Egypt faced arrest for criticizing the government online. Paralegal helped draft a strong declaration and obtain human rights reports.

- **Case 3: LGBTQ+ Persecution**
  Rafael from Honduras faced attacks for being gay. He included affidavits, medical records, and news articles. Granted asylum.

Section 5: Sample Forms and How to Complete

1. **Form I-589: Application for Asylum**
   - Biographic information
   - Detailed statement of persecution
   - Evidence list (documents, witnesses)
2. All immigration forms—including I-589, I-765 (work permit), and related motions or appeals—**must be filed correctly, truthfully, and on time**. Mistakes or delays can lead to automatic denials, missed deadlines, or even deportation.
   Always keep copies of all documents submitted and request proof of receipt when filing.
3. **Checklist for Supporting Documents**
   - Personal affidavit
   - Country conditions reports
   - Medical/psychological records
   - Police or incident reports
   - Letters from witnesses

Section 6: Preparation Tips for Legal Professionals

1. **Paralegal Roles**
    - Assist in drafting personal declarations
    - Help complete I-589
    - Organize evidence and exhibits
    - Translate and format documents

2. **Attorney Roles**
    - Legal strategy and direct representation
    - Prepare clients for testimony
    - Cross-examine government experts

Section 7: Common Mistakes or Misconceptions

- Believing asylum automatically leads to a green card
- Filing too late without showing exception
- Inconsistent testimony
- Not understanding what qualifies as a "particular social group"

- Thinking of any danger qualifies (must be on protected grounds)

Section 8: Legal Strategies and Best Practices

1. **Credible Declaration**
    - Must be vivid, consistent, and emotional but factual
2. **Corroborating Evidence**
    - Support the claim with outside documentation, including expert affidavits
3. **Backup Relief**
    - Always include Withholding of Removal and CAT if applicable
4. **Country Research**
    - Present recent and credible sources of persecution in the home country
5. **Witness Statements**
    - Family or friends confirming abuse, fear, or danger

Section 9: FAQ (Real Detainee Questions)

Q: Can I apply for asylum if I've been here more than a year?

A: Yes, but you must show changed or extraordinary circumstances.

Q: What if I don't have any documents?
A: A strong, consistent affidavit may be enough, but outside support helps.

Q: Can I win without a lawyer?
A: It is possible but very hard. You should at least seek help from a paralegal or legal aid group.

Section 10: National Legal Aid Organizations

- **RAICES** – Texas-based, nationwide asylum support – www.raicestexas.org
- **Human Rights First** – Pro bono asylum work – www.humanrightsfirst.org
- **Asylum Seeker Advocacy Project (ASAP)** – Online legal help – www.asylumadvocacy.org
- **National Immigrant Justice Center (NIJC)** – Legal help in major cities – www.immigrantjustice.org
- **Catholic Legal Immigration Network (CLINIC)** – National nonprofit support – www.cliniclegal.org

Filing Correctly Matters
All immigration forms—including I-589, I-765 (work permit), and related motions or appeals—**must be**

filed correctly, truthfully, and on time. Mistakes or delays can lead to automatic denials, missed deadlines, or even deportation.
Always keep copies of all documents submitted and request proof of receipt when filing.

How Paralegals and Attorneys Help

- **Paralegals** can assist by organizing documents, preparing affidavits, explaining procedures, and helping fill out forms under supervision.
- **Attorneys** provide legal advice, represent clients in court, and strategize defenses. They understand complex legal standards and are essential in high-risk or complicated cases. Working with both can improve the quality of your case and avoid unnecessary mistakes.

Section 7: Common Mistakes & Misconceptions

- **Waiting too long to file**: Many think they can file "whenever," but missing the one-year deadline can be fatal to your case.
- **Thinking fear of poverty or general crime qualifies for asylum**: It must be linked to protected grounds.

- **Relying on bad advice**: Notarios, fake legal advisors, or friends may give false hope or incorrect information.
- **Believing asylum guarantees a green card**: Asylum is only the first step; further applications are needed for permanent residency.

Section 8: Legal Strategies & Best Practices

- Gather **credible evidence**: medical reports, police records, news articles, personal declarations.
- Secure **witness affidavits** and expert statements if possible.
- Stay consistent in your story throughout every interview or form.
- Hire or consult with an experienced **immigration attorney or accredited representative**.
- Keep track of **court dates, deadlines, and receipts**.

Section 9: Legal Aid Resources and Organizations for Asylum Seekers

- **RAICES** – Texas-based nonprofit offering free legal help to immigrants and asylum seekers.

- **Human Rights First** – Provides free legal representation for asylum seekers.
- **American Immigration Council** – Offers legal resources and supports advocacy.
- **International Refugee Assistance Project (IRAP)** – Legal and policy advocacy for displaced individuals.
- **Asylum Seeker Advocacy Project (ASAP)** – Gives support and legal guidance to families seeking asylum.
  These organizations can guide you, provide legal help, or connect you to an attorney if you cannot afford one.

Remember: Asylum is complex, and the stakes are high. Even if you cannot afford a private attorney, many organizations and trained paralegals can assist with preparation to give you the best chance at success.

Real life situation & General Advice

Testimony of real-life experience. The name of the person who had this traumatic experience will not be exposed in this book, but his situation and how he handled it will be.

“I just was arrested by ICE at work, suddenly detained, mistreated, and silenced from communicating with my family. I was facing this situation, scared, alone, and denied basic rights like a phone call for two days—my first internal response was shock and confusion. My mind was racing: *Why me? What just happened? Where am I going? Is my family, okay?* I felt powerless. Then fear set in, especially considering what was next. Thinking about what I had already experienced. The trauma of fleeing danger to get here. Being mistreated by officers who were supposed to uphold the law shook my sense of safety even more. It even triggered memories of past abuse or persecution. I felt humiliated, angry, and deeply anxious, not just for myself but for my loved ones.”

Advice from a practical standpoint, here’s what you should *do* if faced with the same or similar situations. Do your best to stay strong emotionally and mentally:

- **Focus on survival and documentation.** Even while scared, I would try to remember everything—names, badge numbers, time of day, what was said, how I was handled. That’s hard under trauma, but documenting mistreatment could help later.
- **Mentally prepare for legal action.** I’d try to stay calm and remind myself: *This is temporary. I need to survive it so I can fight it.* Whether through asylum, a motion to

suppress, or complaints to oversight agencies, I'd want to hold those officers accountable.

- **Hold onto identity.**
  When you're treated like you don't matter, it's easy to internalize that. I would have to remind myself: *I am human. I have dignity. I have a story. And I'm going to tell it when the time comes.*

- **Faith or hope as anchors.**
  If I had any spiritual beliefs, I'd lean on them hard. And if not, I'd anchor myself in the idea that there are still people out there—maybe a lawyer, a paralegal, an advocate—who will help me fight.

Chapter 6: While in ICE Custody: Preparing for the Next Step

Being held in ICE custody can feel overwhelming, but it's crucial to remain proactive and informed. Here are practical steps to take while detained to protect your rights and prepare for what's next—whether it's release, deportation, or legal relief:

1. **Know Your Status and Case Type**
    - **Determine if you have a removal (deportation) case** or are being held pending immigration proceedings.
    - Request a copy of the **Notice to Appear (NTA)** to understand the charges against you.
2. **Request Legal Help**
    - Ask the facility staff for a list of **pro bono (free) immigration attorneys** or contact a trusted person outside to help locate legal aid.
    - **You have the right to an attorney**, but ICE does not provide one—you must hire or find your own.
3. **Document Everything**
    - Keep a **notebook** with dates, names, and details of your ICE interactions, court hearings, or issues with detention.
    - This record can support any complaints or legal motions in the future.
4. **Request Bond or Parole**
    - You may be eligible for **bond or parole** depending on your case and immigration history.
    - Request a **bond hearing** or ask your attorney to file a motion to review detention status.

5. **Collect and Prepare Documents**

- Gather or request copies of **birth certificates, passports, immigration applications, green card, work permits, and any criminal case documents**.
- These will be crucial for your attorney, any potential relief applications, or release efforts.

6. **Stay in Contact with Family**

- Provide your family with your **A-number** (Alien Registration Number) so they can locate you using ICE's **Online Detainee Locator System**.
- Ask them to assist in gathering documents or seeking legal help on your behalf.

7. **Identify Possible Relief**

Depending on your background, you may qualify for relief from removal:

- **Asylum, Withholding of Removal, or CAT protection** if you fear returning to your home country.
- **Cancellation of Removal** for long-term residents.
- **U-visa, T-visa, VAWA relief** for victims of crimes, trafficking, or abuse.
- **Adjustment of Status** if you have a U.S. citizen spouse or child.

8. Know Your Rights in Detention

- You **do not have to sign any documents** without understanding them.
- You have the right to **remain silent** and to **refuse deportation** until you've had a chance to speak with a lawyer or see an immigration judge.
- You can **file grievances** about mistreatment or medical neglect.

9. Stay Mentally and Physically Strong

- Keep a routine—exercise, read, and stay informed.
- Participate in available **legal orientation programs** or classes

10. Prepare for Immigration Court

- **Understand the process**: Most detainees go before an Immigration Judge. Your first hearing is a **Master Calendar Hearing**, where you'll confirm your identity, the charges, and whether you need time to find a lawyer.
- After that comes the **Merits Hearing**, where the judge will decide your case based on the facts and legal arguments.
- **Practice answering questions** respectfully, clearly, and honestly. Never guess if you don't

know—say “I don’t know” or “I’d like to speak with an attorney first.”

11. Avoid Signing Voluntary Departure Without Understanding

- Officers may offer you voluntary departure to avoid prolonged detention.
- **Don’t sign anything under pressure.** Voluntary departure may hurt your future chances of returning legally. Talk to a lawyer first.

12. Use the Law Library and Legal Orientation Programs (LOPs)

- Most detention centers offer access to legal resources. Use the **law library** to research your case.
- Enroll in a **Legal Orientation Program**, if available—they provide group info sessions on court procedures and available forms of relief.

13. Plan for All Outcomes

Whether you're released, win relief, or face removal:

- **If released**: Make sure you know your next court date, check your address is updated with the court, and follow up with your lawyer.
- **If facing deportation**: Begin planning with loved ones. Notify them early and prepare a

plan for your safe arrival in your home country, including shelter and medication if needed.

- **If you win relief**: You may qualify to remain in the U.S. legally. Follow through on next steps like receiving your green card or work permit.

14. Build a Support Network

- **Reach out to community-based organizations, faith groups, or immigration advocates**. They often provide moral support, legal help, and reentry resources.
- Give your family or support system a **list of key contacts**: attorney, caseworker, or consulate info.

15. File Complaints if Needed

- If you're mistreated, denied medical care, or denied access to legal materials:
    - File a **written grievance** at the facility.
    - Report to the **Office of the Inspector General (OIG)** or the **Civil Rights Division of DHS**.
    - Keep copies and notes about what happened and when.

Chapter 7: Preparing Family and Reentry Plans in Case of Deportation

Facing the possibility of deportation is painful, especially when you have loved ones depending on you in the U.S. But being prepared doesn't mean giving up—it means protecting your family, your dignity, and your future. This chapter is your guide to planning ahead and staying empowered, even through separation.

1. Talk to Your Family Early

- Be honest with your spouse, children, or trusted relatives about what's happening.
- Let them know what to expect, especially emotionally and financially.
- Involve them in your planning where appropriate—don't leave them in the dark.

2. Establish Emergency Legal Authority

- Draft a **Power of Attorney** giving someone you trust the right to handle:
    - Bank accounts
    - Childcare and school decisions
    - Housing, vehicles, and property
- You may need to assign **temporary guardianship** if you have minor children.

- These documents should be notarized and accessible.

3. Secure Important Documents

Make sure your family has copies of:

- Your passport, birth certificate, green card or visa
- Marriage certificate, children's birth certificates
- Tax documents, proof of address, employment history
- Your A-number and ICE case info Store these in a fireproof folder or secure digital file.

4. Financial Preparation

- Add a trusted person to your bank accounts if needed.
- List all your monthly bills—rent, phone, insurance, etc.—so someone can manage them.
- Talk to your employer about final pay or benefits.
- Set up a basic **budget** your family can follow in your absence.

5. School, Health & Community Support

- Inform your children's school if someone new will be picking them up or acting as guardian.

- Make sure your family knows how to access healthcare or prescriptions.
- Reach out to churches, community orgs, or mutual aid groups that provide help to families of the detained or deported.

6. Prepare for Reentry in Your Country

- Contact your consulate to discuss documents, travel, and any return support.
- Identify a safe place to go—relatives, shelters, or organizations that assist deportees.
- If you have medical conditions, work with ICE or your lawyer to plan ahead for continuity of care.

7. Mental and Emotional Support

- Deportation can tear families apart emotionally. Encourage counseling or therapy when possible—especially for children.
- Write letters, record messages, or create a binder for your kids so they feel connected even if you're separated.

8. Stay in Contact After Deportation

- Give your family your future address, email, or a reliable contact person.
- Use social media, WhatsApp, or calling cards to stay connected.

- Stay involved in your case if you're planning to file a **Motion to Reopen** later on.

Chapter 8: Appeals and Motions to Reopen

"The fight isn't over just because they said it's over."

When a removal (deportation) order is issued against you, it is not necessarily the final word. U.S. immigration law offers two critical legal remedies: **Appeals** and **Motions to Reopen or Reconsider**. These tools can help correct legal errors, present new evidence, or challenge unfair decisions.

◆ 1. Understanding the Appeal Process

If an immigration judge rules against you, you have the right to appeal that decision to the **Board of Immigration Appeals (BIA)**.

✓ What You Need to Know:

- **Deadline**: You must file a *Notice of Appeal* (Form EOIR-26) within **30 days** of the immigration judge's decision.
- You do **not** need full legal arguments on day one—just a summary of why you're appealing.
- Once accepted, you'll get a briefing schedule. This is when you (or your attorney) submit a **legal brief** explaining why the judge got it wrong—facts, law, or both.

✓ **What the BIA Looks At:**

- Legal errors the judge made
- Misinterpretation of facts
- Whether due process was violated (example: you didn't have a fair chance to present your case)

✓ **Outcome Possibilities:**

- **Affirmed**: The judge's decision stands.
- **Reversed**: You win—case may be terminated or remanded.
- **Remanded**: Sent back to the immigration judge for more hearings.

📚 **Case Example:**
INS v. Elias-Zacarias, *502 U.S. 478 (1992)*

- This case involved a Guatemalan man who refused to join a guerrilla group and claimed asylum. The Supreme Court ruled against him but clarified the importance of properly interpreting asylum claims and the legal standards required during appeals.

◆ **2. Filing a Motion to Reopen**

Even after a deportation order, if new facts or evidence come up, you can ask the court to "reopen" the case.

✓ **When to Use This:**

- You couldn't present certain facts before due to exceptional circumstances.
- You now qualify for relief that you didn't before (e.g., asylum due to changed country conditions, marriage to a U.S. citizen, new visa eligibility).
- Your prior lawyer messed up your case (**ineffective assistance of counsel**).
- Your case was conducted without your knowledge (**in absentia removal**).

✓ **Basic Requirements:**

- Must be filed within **90 days** of the final order—unless you claim an exception.
- Include:
  - A detailed affidavit explaining the reason
  - New evidence or documents
  - If based on ineffective assistance, include a **Lozada affidavit** showing you contacted or tried to report the former attorney.
- **Key Forms:**

- *Form EOIR-29*: If filing with USCIS.
- *Form EOIR-26B*: If filing with the BIA.

📚 **Case Example:**
Matter of Lozada, *19 I&N Dec. 637 (BIA 1988)*

- This case established the procedure for claiming ineffective assistance of counsel. You must meet strict requirements under *Lozada* to successfully reopen your case based on your attorney's poor performance.

3. Motions to Reconsider

A **motion to reconsider** asks the same court to review its decision because you believe the judge applied the law incorrectly or failed to consider key evidence.

- **Deadline to File:**
  Within **30 days** of the final decision.
- **Common Use Cases:**
  - Legal arguments were misunderstood or misapplied.
  - Important evidence was overlooked or misinterpreted.

Why the Power of Attorney Is Important During Immigration Proceedings

Immigration proceedings, especially those involving detention, deportation, or removal—can happen quickly and with little warning. A **Power of Attorney (POA)** is a legal document that allows a trusted person (the "agent") to act on behalf of the individual (the "principal") in managing personal, financial, and legal affairs.

This is especially helpful when the immigrant might be **detained by ICE**, transferred to another facility, or **removed from the country**.

✅ **Benefits of Having a Power of Attorney**

1. **Protecting Personal Property**
   A POA allows a family member to legally manage the immigrant's property (home, car, bank accounts, pets, etc.), avoiding loss or abandonment.

2. **Managing Financial Responsibilities**
   The agent can pay rent, utilities, child support, or other bills to prevent late fees, repossession, or eviction.

3. **Caring for Children or Dependents**
   If the immigrant has children or elderly dependents, a POA can allow a family member to make medical, educational, and emergency decisions.

4. **Making Legal Decisions if Deported**
   The agent can sell property, close accounts,

retrieve stored items, or represent the person's interests after removal.

5. **Peace of Mind**
   Knowing that a trusted person can act on your behalf reduces stress and helps focus on the legal battle ahead.

⚠️ Potential Drawbacks of a Power of Attorney

1. **Risk of Misuse**
   If the person chosen is not trustworthy, they could misuse funds, sell property, or make decisions that aren't in your best interest.
2. **Loss of Control**
   Granting POA means giving someone legal control over your assets—temporarily giving up full control yourself.
3. **Limited Scope (if not carefully written)**
   A poorly written POA may not include all necessary powers or could expire at the wrong time. It's important the document is tailored to the immigrant's specific needs.
4. **State and Legal Requirements Vary**
   Some institutions may not accept a POA unless it's notarized, or they may have their own forms, especially for bank accounts or real estate transactions.

✅ **Best Practices**

1. **Choose someone trustworthy**—a close family member or friend with a proven track record of responsibility.
2. **Work with a qualified legal professional** to draft the POA to fit the immigrant's specific needs (property, banking, children, legal matters, etc.).
3. **Limit the POA's duration or scope** if necessary—for example, only allowing certain actions and for a set period.

Special Considerations

- **Filing a Stay of Removal:**
  Filing an appeal or motion does **not automatically stop removal**. You must request a **stay of removal** to prevent deportation while your case is under review.
- **Exception for Changed Country Conditions:**
  If you miss the 90-day deadline for a motion to reopen, you may still file if you can prove that conditions in your home country have worsened after your case concluded.

📚 **Case Example:**

Matter of S-Y-G, *24 I&N Dec. 247 (BIA 2007)*

- The BIA outlined how to establish changed country conditions, allowing individuals to reopen their cases beyond the standard 90-day limit when new dangers arise in their home country.

Final Steps and Advice

1. **Consult with a Qualified Immigration Attorney or Accredited Representative.**
   Professional guidance can make the difference between success and failure.
2. **Act Quickly.**
   Immigration law imposes strict deadlines. Missing them can permanently close doors.
3. **Ensure Proper Filing.**
   Submit the correct forms and include strong supporting documents.
4. **Request a Stay of Removal if Needed.**
   Don't assume your deportation will be paused—**you must file for a stay** to remain in the U.S. while your case is pending.

Sample 1: Motion to Reopen Removal Proceedings (Based on New Evidence)

[Your Name]
[Alien Registration Number (A#)]
[Your Address]

To:
Executive Office for Immigration Review
[Name of Immigration Court or BIA]
[Address of the Court]

Re: Motion to Reopen Removal Proceedings
Case Number: [Case Number]
Date of Final Order: [Date]

Honorable Immigration Judge,

Pursuant to **8 C.F.R. § 1003.23(b)(3)**, I respectfully submit this **Motion to Reopen Removal Proceedings** based on new and material evidence that was not available at the time of my original hearing.

Grounds for Motion:

1. **New Evidence of Changed Country Conditions:**
   Since the date of the final removal order on [Date], conditions in my home country of [Country] have significantly worsened. [Provide a brief explanation: e.g., "A recent surge in targeted violence against ethnic minorities has placed me at serious risk of harm if removed."]

2. **Supporting Evidence:**

   - News Article: *[Title, Date]*

   - Human Rights Report: *[Title, Organization]*

- Affidavit of [Witness or Expert, if any]
- Personal Declaration Attached

I respectfully request that this Honorable Court grant this Motion to Reopen and consider the attached evidence in support of my claim for [Asylum, Withholding of Removal, or other relief].

Request for Stay of Removal:

I also respectfully request a **stay of removal** pending the outcome of this motion.

Thank you for your time and consideration.

Respectfully submitted,

[Signature]
[Printed Name]
[Date]

Sample 2: Notice of Appeal to the Board of Immigration Appeals (Form EOIR-26 Sample Content)

Board of Immigration Appeals
Office of the Clerk
5107 Leesburg Pike, Suite 2000
Falls Church, VA 22041

Notice of Appeal from a Decision of an Immigration Judge

- **Respondent Name:** [Your Full Name]
- **Alien Registration Number (A#):** [A Number]
- **Case Number:** [Case Number]
- **Date of IJ Decision:** [Date]

Grounds for Appeal:
I am appealing the Immigration Judge's decision issued on [Date], which ordered my removal from the United States. I believe the Immigration Judge made errors in the application of immigration law and failed to consider critical evidence, including [briefly mention the error, e.g., "evidence of my credible fear of persecution and eligibility for asylum."].

I respectfully request that the Board of Immigration Appeals review my case and reverse the removal order.

Relief Requested:
Reversal of the Immigration Judge's decision and remand for further proceedings.

Respectfully submitted,

[Signature]
[Printed Name]
[Date]

Remember, although the immigration system may feel overwhelming, legal remedies exist. Understanding and exercising your rights is the first step toward protecting your future.

📌 Additional Things You Need to Know (Strategy Tip for Adopted Individuals Facing Deportation)

If you were adopted and brought to the United States as a child, there may be a powerful legal strategy available that could protect you from removal or deportation – even if you have a criminal record or prior immigration issues.

Here's what you need to understand:

Under The Child Citizenship Act of 2000 (CCA), certain adopted children automatically became U.S. citizens if they met specific conditions before turning 18. This is especially important for those who were adopted before their 16th birthday.

The law went into effect on February 27, 2001, and it automatically grants U.S. citizenship to adopted children if all of the following apply:

1. You were under age 18 on February 27, 2001.
2. You were lawfully admitted as a permanent resident (green card holder).
3. You were residing in the U.S. in the legal and physical custody of your U.S. citizen parent(s).

4. You were adopted before turning 16 (or by 18 if part of a sibling group).

☞ If you met those conditions before February 27, 2001, you may already be a U.S. citizen automatically by law – even if you were never issued a Certificate of Citizenship.
In that case, you should NOT be subject to deportation and may be able to file a motion to terminate removal proceedings or a motion to reopen, depending on your current legal status.

☞ If you were over 18 on February 27, 2001, or didn't meet all requirements before that date, you may still be eligible to apply for naturalization, but you must file a formal application through USCIS.

This strategy becomes important when filing a cancellation of removal or a motion to reopen based on the fact that you should have received automatic citizenship but never got the paperwork. This could be the key to stopping your deportation.

▤ Strategic Filing Tip:
If your case involves an adoption and you were under age 16 at the time, always investigate whether the CCA applies. A qualified immigration attorney or paralegal can help verify whether you automatically gained citizenship, even if you were never issued a document proving it.

This is one of the most overlooked but powerful strategies in immigration defense for adopted individuals.

🔚 Conclusion

Having a Power of Attorney during immigration proceedings isn't just about protecting property—it's about protecting your **life, family, and future**. It's a smart move that can help ensure things are taken care of if you're detained or removed, as long as it's done carefully and with the right safeguards in place.

✊ Final Words

Even after removal, injustice can be challenged. This system may be cruel, but it's not unbeatable. Appeals and motions to reopen are legal tools designed for people with the strength to keep going, even when others have given up. **Use them wisely.**

You don't have to accept the end as the end. Sometimes it's just the next move.

RICK CURRY: Author
Accused Federal Guide to Justice Paralegal Services LLC
P.O. Box 260
Rex, GA 30273
accusedme23@gmail.com

This material is provided for **educational and informational purposes only**. It is not intended to serve as legal advice. Readers are encouraged to consult with a qualified legal professional for any legal matters related to their case or circumstances.

■ Immigration Survival Glossary

Essential Terms for Navigating ICE Custody and Removal Proceedings

A

A-Number (Alien Registration Number)
A unique identification number assigned to non-citizens by the U.S. government for immigration tracking purposes.

Adjustment of Status
The legal process that allows a non-citizen to apply for lawful permanent residency without leaving the United States.

Asylum
Protection offered to individuals who fear persecution in their home country due to race, religion, nationality, political opinion, or membership in a particular social group.

B

Bond Hearing
A proceeding before an immigration judge to determine whether a detained immigrant can be released while their case is pending, and if so, at what cost.

C

Cancellation of Removal
A form of immigration relief that allows certain non-citizens to remain in the U.S. and adjust status to lawful permanent resident if strict eligibility criteria are met.

Consular Processing
Applying for a visa or lawful status from a U.S. consulate or embassy outside the country.

D

Deportation (Removal)
The legal process of being expelled from the United States due to immigration or criminal violations.

Detainer (ICE Hold)
A request from ICE to local authorities to continue holding a person in custody so ICE can assume control.

E

EWI (Entry Without Inspection)
Entering the United States without authorization or passing through a designated inspection checkpoint.

F

Fair Use (Copyright Law)
A legal exception allowing limited use of copyrighted material without permission for educational, commentary, or research purposes under U.S. law.

Form I-213
An ICE document summarizing how an individual was apprehended and why they are considered deportable.

G

Green Card
A common term for the Permanent Resident Card that proves lawful permanent resident status in the U.S.

H

Hearing Notice (Notice of Hearing)
An official court notice providing the date, time, and location of an immigration hearing.

I

ICE (Immigration and Customs Enforcement)
The federal agency responsible for enforcing immigration laws, including arrests, detentions, and deportations.

I-862 (Notice to Appear)
The document issued to start removal proceedings, listing allegations and legal grounds for deportation.

Immigration Court
A specialized administrative court where immigration judges decide removal cases and applications for relief.

L

Legal Permanent Resident (LPR)
A non-citizen granted the legal right to live and work in the United States on a permanent basis.

M

Motion to Reopen
A request to reexamine an immigration case that has already been decided, typically based on new evidence or changed circumstances.

P

Parole
Temporary permission to enter or remain in the U.S. granted for urgent humanitarian reasons or significant public benefit.

Power of Attorney (POA)
A legal document allowing someone else to act on your behalf for financial, legal, or family-related matters.

R

Relief from Removal
Any legal strategy or application that can prevent or delay deportation, including asylum and cancellation of removal.

S

Stay of Removal
A temporary delay of deportation, often granted while a case or appeal is still pending.

T

Temporary Protected Status (TPS)
A humanitarian status granted to individuals from countries experiencing armed conflict, natural disasters, or other temporary crises.

V

Voluntary Departure
Permission to leave the U.S. on your own terms and at your own expense, allowing you to avoid a formal removal order.

About the Author & Dedicated Contacts

Rick Curry
Author & Owner of Accused Federal Guide to Justice Paralegal LLC

With over 25 years of experience in federal criminal law, Rick Curry is a certified paralegal and a passionate advocate for freedom, justice, and equality. As a former federally convicted felon who has turned his life around, Rick offers a unique and powerful perspective to those facing challenges within the federal system.

Through his company, he provides legal guidance and support to individuals navigating the complexities of indictments, sentencing, appeals, and post-conviction relief.

Rick is also a published author and creative storyteller. His works include:

- The Accused Federal Guide to Justice Handbook (Criminal Defense Techniques)
- Asylum (Immigration Defense Techniques)
- The Five Pups of the Hidden Land of Buganda (Family Fiction Series)
- Implied Malice (Urban Novel)
- Malice Afterthought(Pt 2 Urban Novel)

His writing bridges the gap between law, advocacy, and storytelling, educating, entertaining, and inspiring change.

The author, Rick Curry, appreciates all his readers and supporters.

Contact Information

□ **Mailing Address:**
P.O. Box 260
Rex, GA 30273-9998

Phone: (770) 334-5180 Email:
accusedme23@gmail.com

Made in the USA
Monee, IL
16 November 2025

34962447R00056